Creating Cut-Up Sentence Books

An Effective Multi-Sensory Strategy to Develop Reading Skills

by
Kathryn Stroh

illustrated by
Julie Anderson

Publisher
Key Education Publishing Company, LLC
Minneapolis, Minnesota 55431

CONGRATULATIONS ON YOUR PURCHASE OF A KEY EDUCATION PRODUCT!

The editors at Key Education are former teachers who bring experience, enthusiasm, and quality to each and every product. Thousands of teachers have looked to the staff at Key Education for new and innovative resources to make their work more enjoyable and rewarding. Key Education is committed to developing and publishing educational materials that will assist teachers in building a strong and developmentally appropriate curriculum for young children.

PLAN FOR GREAT TEACHING EXPERIENCES WHEN YOU USE
EDUCATIONAL MATERIALS FROM KEY EDUCATION PUBLISHING COMPANY, LLC.

About The Author

Kathryn Stroh has received a bachelor of science in child development, a masters degree in education, and is a certified Reading Recovery® instructor. She has taught for eleven years with experiences in special education, kindergarten, first grade, second grade, and she has taught literacy groups for at-risk students. Kathryn lives in Lodi, California with her husband *(who also teaches)* and their two young children.

This book is lovingly dedicated to my mom— my mentor. Love, Katy

Credits

Author: Kathryn B. Stroh
Project Director: Sherrill B. Flora
Editor: Kelly Huxmann
Art Director: Mary Clair
Inside Illustrations: Julie Anderson
Cover Design: Mary Eden

Key Education welcomes manuscripts and product ideas from teachers. For a copy of our submission guidelines, please send a self-addressed, stamped envelope to:

Key Education Publishing Company, LLC
Acquisitions Department
9601 Newton Avenue South
Minneapolis, Minnesota 55431

Standard Book Number: 1-933052-13-9
Creating Cut-Up Sentence Books
Copyright © 2005 Key Education Publishing Company, LLC
Minneapolis, Minnesota 55431

Contents

Introduction

The hands-on reading activity of assembling "cut-up" or "mixed-up" sentences is a strategy that has been well documented as an effective tool for teaching young children how to read. This approach is currently being utilized by a wide variety of reading philosophies and practices. It has been integrated into many of the most prominent basal reading programs and is considered an essential activity in the prescribed lessons of the Reading Recovery® program. It can also be found in the Four-Blocks® Literacy Model. If you think back, you may even remember that when you were in school you assembled mixed-up words to create meaningful sentences.

This is an old theory that has been proven to be effective — not to mention a great deal of fun for children. Learning to read while getting to talk, listen, look, cut, color, and paste makes this a wonderful multi-sensory experience that helps meet the needs of a wide variety of ability levels and learning styles.

Cut-up sentence activities also assist children in meeting many of the national and state reading standards established for kindergarten and first grade. Children will also develop skills and strategies that will assist them in comprehending, evaluating, interpreting, and appreciating what they read.

When children are presented with cut-up sentence activities, they are provided opportunities to practice many different skills:

- one-to-one correspondence between the spoken and written word

- understanding left to right directionality

- understanding return sweep

- locating capital and lowercase letters identified by a period or question mark

- distinguishing letters from words

- reading high-frequency words

- connecting experiences to text and using sentences to share information

- English Language Learners (ELL) can also practice common English sentence structures through cut-up sentence activities.

The procedures outlined on the following pages (pages 5 and 6), together with the reproducible cut-up sentence books, will provide your students with fun, successful, and effective experiences to help develop their reading skills and strategies.

Creating Cut-Up Sentence Books

The reproducible cut-up sentence books found in *Creating Cut-Up Sentence Books* were designed around the most popular themes taught in kindergarten. Each book can be presented as a whole group activity — by having each child contribute a page to create one large classroom book — or as an individual activity in which all of the students make their own cut-up sentence books.

Whole Group Activity

1. Choose one of the stories. Write each word from the story on an **index card** *(one word per card)*.
2. Read the words together, making sure that you read them out of order. Discuss how the words do not make any sense.
3. Randomly hand out the cards to individual students.
4. Have the students place the cards in proper sequence in a pocket chart. Practice reading the sentence each time a word is added to help establish the meaning of the sentence.
5. At this stage, decide whether the children will make their own books or if they will create one whole classroom book. Then follow the procedures described below for creating the pages.

Individual Procedures

1. If you use **table or center rotations**, the cut-up sentence activity can be one of the table rotations. Alternatively, children may simply work at tables at the same time.
2. Each child should have an **envelope labeled with his or her name**. The envelope can be reused for each story. Put the **words from the cut-up sentence** inside the envelope. You can precut the words or give the children copies of the sentence and have them cut out the words themselves.
3. Have the children **place the words faceup** on the table and attempt to **arrange the sentence** without a model. Children can check their work by looking at the classroom sentence that is in the pocket chart. Incorrect sentences can be corrected.
4. Provide each child with a **Level 1, 2, or 3 reproducible page** according to individual abilities. *(Reproducible pages are included for each story. See the examples below.)*

    Level 1 *(easiest)*: The child glues the cut-up words on top of the words on the page.
    Level 2 *(difficult)*: The child glues the cut-up words below the words on the page.
    Level 3 *(most difficult)*: The child glues the cut-up words on the page in proper order without any model.

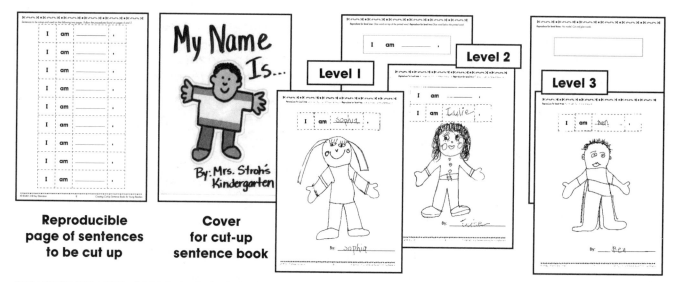

Reproducible page of sentences to be cut up   **Cover for cut-up sentence book**   Level 1   Level 2   Level 3

5. Have each child draw and color a picture to **illustrate the sentence**. In order to encourage the matching of text with pictures, the illustration can be completed before the cut-up words are glued in place. Alternatively, you may choose to use the **picture cards** included with each story. *(See Step 6 for more information.)*

6. There are several ways to help the children complete the **fill-in-the-blank** spaces. As a class, brainstorm ideas and print the children's responses on the board, index cards, or chart paper. Another fun idea is to provide the children with picture cards that have the words printed on them. The children can choose which picture cards they want to use to finish their sentences. Each cut-up sentence story in this book (except Theme 1) has a set of picture cards that can be reproduced for the children to use.

7. The finished pages can be compiled into a whole **classroom cut-up sentence book** that the children will enjoy reading over and over again. Each child can also create several pages with different fill-in-the-blank responses and bind them together to create an **individual cut-up sentence book**.

8. Each story comes with a piece of reproducible art that the children can use to make **book covers**. Copy the pattern for each of the children. Each child can color, cut out, and glue the finished pattern to a piece of construction paper to create the cover. Have the child print the name of the book and his or her own name on the cover.

9. The cut-up sentence activities presented in this book offer children repeated practice reading **high-frequency words**, as well as strengthening all of the skills and strategies listed on page 4. The high-frequency words that are used have been selected from standards-based programs.

THE FIRST 25 WORD LIST

I	the	on	see	in	my	like	at	look	to	and	go	it
is	here	you	for	have	said	can	play	she	are	he	they	

Ideas for Authentic Assessment

The following ideas will provide the teacher with assessment techniques to document skills and a student's progress utilizing cut-up sentence activities.

1. Use the following example sentences labeled for the beginning, middle, or end of the year. Reproduce enough for the entire class.

    Beginning of the year: I see my mom. I can see the cat.

    Middle of the year: Can you play on this? Look at me play on the ___.

    End of the year: The cows said, "moo." Can you? Here are the cows. They like to ___.

2. The teacher should pre-cut the sentences and place them in an envelope for each student. Have the children work on assembling the sentences independently.

3. Have each child glue the sentences onto a piece of "blank" paper (no models or grids). This will allow the teacher to observe many skills, such as:
   • Did the child know where to start the sentence?
   • Did the child work from left to right?
   • Was the child able to carry a return sweep to the next line?
   • Did the child begin with a capital letter and end with appropriate punctuation?
   • Did the child's sentence illustration match the meaning of the text?

4. Have each of the children read their finished work.
   • Did the child read the high-frequency words?
   • Was the child able to maintain one-to-one correspondence?
   • Take notes on the back of the page to remind you of key points for that child.

Theme 1: Learning Our Names
High-Frequency Words: I, am

Directions:

1. Refer to the procedures described on pages 5 and 6. Be sure to print each high-frequency word on an **index card** and review the words with the children prior to creating the cut-up sentence book.

2. Copy the **cut-up sentences** *(page 8)* and distribute them to the children in their envelopes.

3. Select the Level 1, 2, or 3 **reproducible book page** *(pages 9 and 10)* for each child. Choose the page according to the ability level of each child. Copy and distribute them to the children.

4. Copy the **book cover pattern** below. Have each child color, cut out, and glue the pattern onto a piece of construction paper. After the inside pages are complete, the cover can be added to finish the book.

5. Copy the reproducible **Person Pattern** *(page 11)* and distribute to the children. The children can use the patterns to draw themselves. Have them color, cut out, and glue the pictures onto their book pages below their cut-out sentences.

Specific Ideas for Theme 1:

◆ This is a wonderful "beginning the school year" book, as well as the perfect book for teaching the concept of cut-up sentences. Always have the children begin in the top left corner of the page so they understand where to begin reading and writing.

◆ Write each child's name on a sentence strip and add his or her photograph. As a group, let the children have fun identifying their names. Place the sentence strips in a pocket chart for the children to use as a reference. Let each child create a page for a classroom "Our Names" book. This book will be enjoyed by the children all year long.

Skills Practiced:

◆ Knowing where to start and which way to go
◆ Identifying a word vs. a letter

Book cover pattern

Sentences for cut-up sentence book. See directions on page 7.

Theme 1: Learning Our Names

I	am	_____	∎
I	am	_____	∎
I	am	_____	∎
I	am	_____	∎
I	am	_____	∎
I	am	_____	∎
I	am	_____	∎
I	am	_____	∎
I	am	_____	∎

I   am _____ .

By: _____

Level 3: No model. Cut and glue the words in the correct order.

Theme 1: Learning Our Names

By: _____

Person Pattern

Theme 2: How Do You Feel?

High-Frequency Words: I, feel

Directions:

1. Refer to the procedures described on pages 5 and 6. Be sure to print each high-frequency word on an **index card** and review the words with the children prior to creating the cut-up sentence book.

2. Copy the **cut-up sentences** *(page 13)* and distribute them to the children in their envelopes.

3. Select the Level 1, 2, or 3 **reproducible book page** *(pages 14 and 15)* for each child. Choose the page according to the ability level of each child. Copy and distribute them to the children.

4. Copy the **book cover pattern** below. Have each child color, cut out, and glue the pattern onto a piece of construction paper. After the inside pages are complete, the cover can be added to finish the book.

5. Copy and distribute the reproducible **picture cards** *(page 16)*. Let the children use the cards as a reference for spelling and for choosing words to add to their stories. Alternatively, have the children select their own words to complete their stories.

Specific Ideas for Theme 2:

◆ This theme can be a fun classroom book. Have each child create a page that tells how he or she feels. Bind all of the pages together and practice reading them as a group.

◆ Each child may also wish to make a four-page "How Do You Feel?" book with pages illustrating these emotions: happy, sad, mad, and surprised. Provide each child with the picture cards found on page 16. Let each child create a cover for their book and staple the pages together.

Skills Practiced:

◆ Knowing where to start and which way to go
◆ Identifying a word vs. a letter

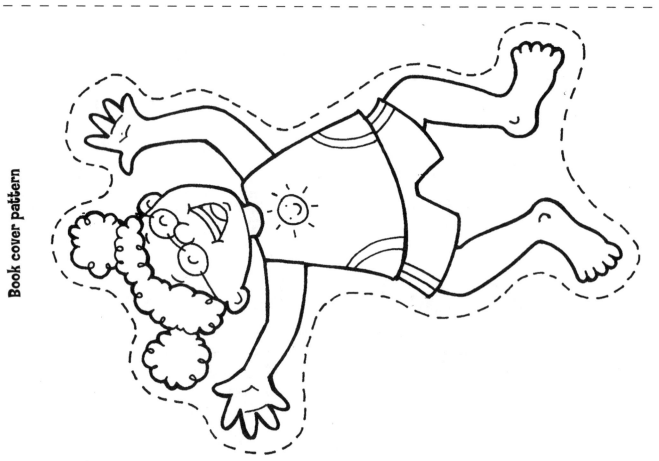

Book cover pattern

I	feel	_____	.
I	feel	_____	.
I	feel	_____	.
I	feel	_____	.
I	feel	_____	.
I	feel	_____	.
I	feel	_____	.
I	feel	_____	.
I	feel	_____	.

By: _____

Level 3: No model. Cut and glue the words in the correct order.   *Theme 2: How Do You Feel?*

By: _____

happy

sad

mad

surprised

Theme 3: My Body Parts
High-Frequency Words: I, see, my

Directions:

1. Refer to the procedures described on pages 5 and 6. Be sure to print each high-frequency word on an **index card** and review the words with the children prior to creating the cut-up sentence book.

2. Copy the **cut-up sentences** *(page 18)* and distribute them to the children in their envelopes.

3. Select the Level 1, 2, or 3 **reproducible book page** *(pages 19 and 20)* for each child. Choose the page according to the ability level of each child. Copy and distribute them to the children.

4. Copy the **book cover pattern** below. Have each child color, cut out, and glue the pattern onto a piece of construction paper. After the inside pages are complete, the cover can be added to finish the book.

5. Copy and distribute the reproducible **picture cards** *(page 21)*. Let the children use the cards as a reference for spelling and for choosing words to add to their stories. Alternatively, have the children select their own words to complete their stories.

Specific Ideas for Theme 3:

◆ Before beginning to work with the high-frequency words and cut-up sentences, have the children take turns looking at their different body parts in a mirror. Then articulate the sentence that the children will be creating. For example, when a child looks in the mirror and holds up his arm, he should say, "I see my arm." The next child may say, "I see my nose," and so on.

◆ The children may illustrate their entire bodies on the book pages, glue on a couple of sentences, and then draw a line from each sentence to the corresponding body part.

Skills Practiced:

◆ Maintaining one-to-one correspondence
◆ Knowing where to start and which way to go
◆ Identifying known words

Book cover pattern

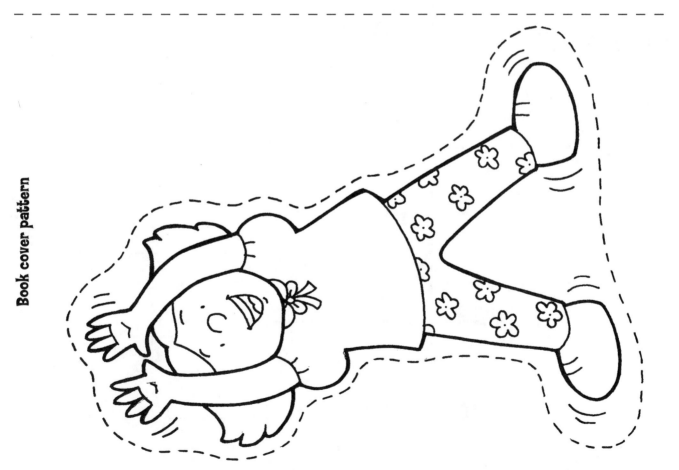

Sentences for cut-up sentence book. See directions on page 17.

Theme 3: My Body Parts

I	see	my	_____	.
I	see	my	_____	.
I	see	my	_____	.
I	see	my	_____	.
I	see	my	_____	.
I	see	my	_____	.
I	see	my	_____	.
I	see	my	_____	.
I	see	my	_____	.

I   see   my _____ **.**

By: _____

Level 3: No model. Cut and glue the words in the correct order.

Theme 3: My Body Parts

By: _____

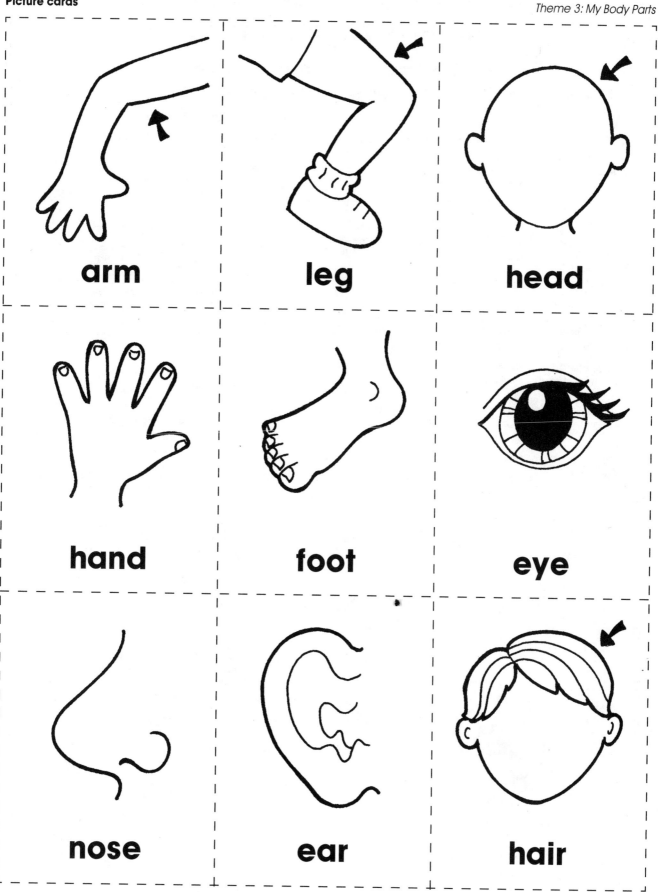

arm

leg

head

hand

foot

eye

nose

ear

hair

Theme 4: My Five Senses

High-Frequency Words: I, can, the

Directions:

1. Refer to the procedures described on pages 5 and 6. Be sure to print each high-frequency word on an **index card** and review the words with the children prior to creating the cut-up sentence book.

2. Copy the **cut-up sentences** *(page 23)* and distribute them to the children in their envelopes.

3. Select the Level 1, 2, or 3 **reproducible book page** *(pages 24 and 25)* for each child. Choose the page according to the ability level of each child. Copy and distribute them to the children.

4. Copy the **book cover pattern** below. Have each child color, cut out, and glue the pattern onto a piece of construction paper. After the inside pages are complete, the cover can be added to finish the book.

5. Copy and distribute the reproducible **picture cards** *(page 26)*. Let the children use the cards as a reference for spelling and for choosing words to add to their stories. Alternatively, have the children select their own words to complete their stories.

Specific Ideas for Theme 4:

◆ Read *The Gingerbread Man*. Have the children help make gingerbread cookies and then discuss the five senses. Ask each of the children to draw a gingerbread man and create these sentences about him:

"I can <u>smell</u> the <u>gingerbread man</u>."
"I can <u>see</u> the <u>gingerbread man</u>."
"I can <u>touch</u> the <u>gingerbread man</u>."
"I can <u>taste</u> the <u>gingerbread man</u>."

◆ Another fun idea for this theme is to create five different classroom books. Divide the children into five different work groups (one for each of the senses). Each group will make a cut-up sentence book for the sense they have been assigned.

Skills Practiced:

◆ Exhibiting a return sweep *(Depending on the time of year this theme is taught, the concept of a return sweep may be difficult for many kindergartners.)*

Book cover pattern

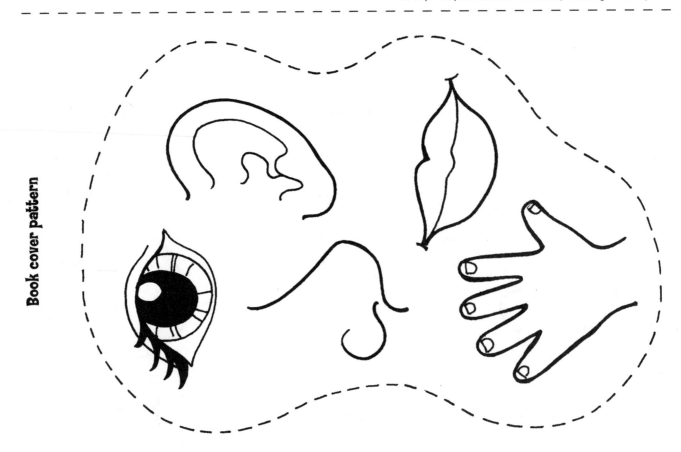

Sentences for cut-up sentence book. See directions on page 22.

Theme 4: My Five Senses

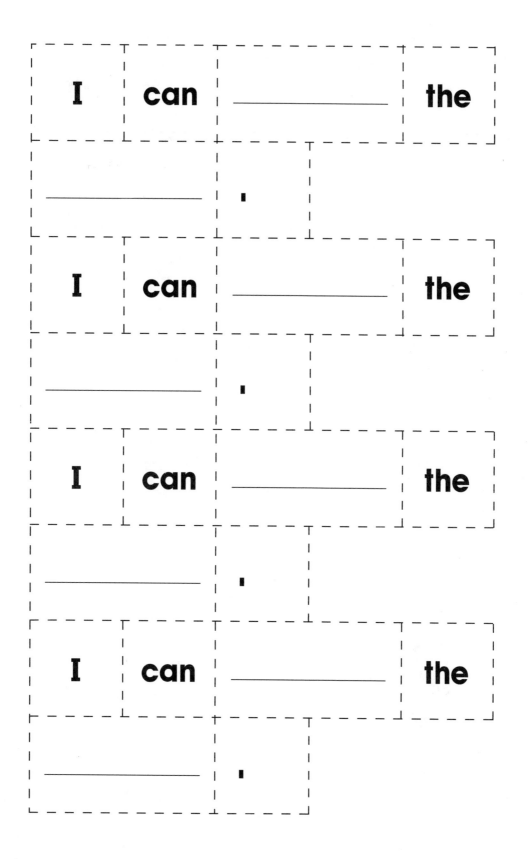

I can _____ the

_____ .

I can _____ the

_____ .

I can _____ the

_____ .

I can _____ the

_____ .

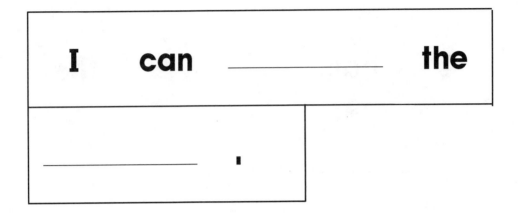
I can _____ the

_____ .

By: _____

Level 3: No model. Cut and glue the words in the correct order.

Theme 4: My Five Senses

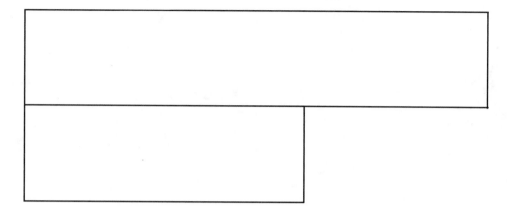

By: _____

see	**hear**	**smell**	**touch**
taste	**sun**	**perfume**	**radio**
finger paint	**ice cream**	**flower**	**drum**

Theme 5: My House

High-Frequency Words: my, house, has, a

Directions:

1. Refer to the procedures described on pages 5 and 6. Be sure to print each high-frequency word on an **index card** and review the words with the children prior to creating the cut-up sentence book.

2. Copy the **cut-up sentences** *(page 28)* and distribute them to the children in their envelopes.

3. Select the Level 1, 2, or 3 **reproducible book page** *(pages 29 and 30)* for each child. Choose the page according to the ability level of each child. Copy and distribute them to the children.

4. Copy the **book cover pattern** below. Have each child color, cut out, and glue the pattern onto a piece of construction paper. After the inside pages are complete, the cover can be added to finish the book.

5. Copy and distribute the reproducible **picture cards** *(page 31)*. Let the children use the cards as a reference for spelling and for choosing words to add to their stories. Alternatively, have the children select their own words to complete their stories.

Specific Ideas for Theme 5:

◆ When teaching this theme, a fun preliminary activity is for the children to draw a large mural of a house. Have them draw lines and label various parts of the house, such as chimney, door, window, and table. The mural can be used as a reference for the children when they are creating their own cut-up sentence books.

◆ The children may also wish to draw their own homes in their books. They can use the cut-up sentences to label some of their favorite rooms or things in their own houses.

◆ The "My House" cut-up sentence book can also be used with numbers, such as 5 windows, 2 doors, or 1 chimney.

Skills Practiced:

◆ Checking beyond the first letter of a word *(Example: house vs. has)*

◆ Maintaining one-to-one correspondence

Book cover pattern

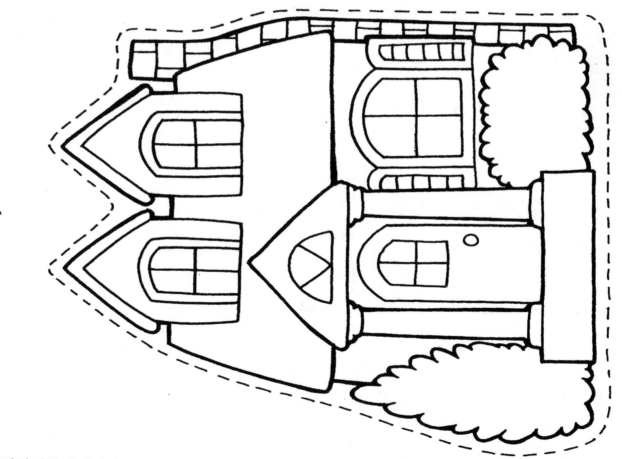

Sentences for cut-up sentence book. See directions on page 27.

My	house	has	a	_____	▪
My	house	has	a	_____	▪
My	house	has	a	_____	▪
My	house	has	a	_____	▪
My	house	has	a	_____	▪
My	house	has	a	_____	▪
My	house	has	a	_____	▪
My	house	has	a	_____	▪
My	house	has	a	_____	▪

Level 1: Glue each word on top of the printed word.
Level 2: Glue each word below the printed word.

My house has a _____ .

By: _____

Level 3: No model. Cut and glue the words in the correct order.

Theme 5: My House

By: _____

kitchen

bathroom

bedroom

living room

Theme 6: I Like To Play

High-Frequency Words: I, like, to, play

Directions:

1. Refer to the procedures described on pages 5 and 6. Be sure to print each high-frequency word on an **index card** and review the words with the children prior to creating the cut-up sentence book.

2. Copy the **cut-up sentences** *(page 33)* and distribute them to the children in their envelopes.

3. Select the Level 1, 2, or 3 **reproducible book page** *(pages 34 and 35)* for each child. Choose the page according to the ability level of each child. Copy and distribute them to the children.

4. Copy the **book cover pattern** below. Have each child color, cut out, and glue the pattern onto a piece of construction paper. After the inside pages are complete, the cover can be added to finish the book.

5. Copy and distribute the reproducible **picture cards** *(page 36)*. Let the children use the cards as a reference for spelling and for choosing words to add to their stories. Alternatively, have the children select their own words to complete their stories.

Specific Ideas for Theme 6:

◆ The theme "I Like to Play" encourages children to think about the types of games they enjoy playing. The picture cards on page 36 will provide the children with examples of team sports and outside games. Before showing the children the picture cards, ask them to brainstorm different types of games that they like to play. Make a list of the games.

◆ Another fun idea to modify this activity is to add the word "with." Write "I like to play with _____." on the board or chart paper. Let the children take turns filling in the blank.

Skills Practiced:

◆ Maintaining one-to-one correspondence
◆ Re-reading to self-monitor

Book cover pattern

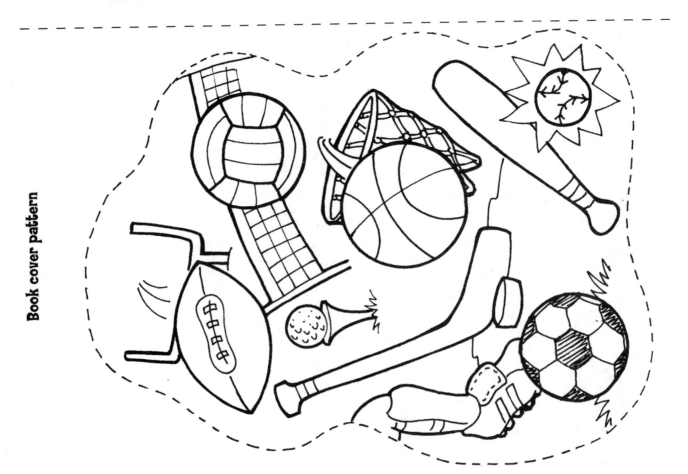

Sentences for cut-up sentence book. See directions on page 32.

Theme 6: I Like to Play

I	like	to	play	_____	.
I	like	to	play	_____	.
I	like	to	play	_____	.
I	like	to	play	_____	.
I	like	to	play	_____	.
I	like	to	play	_____	.
I	like	to	play	_____	.
I	like	to	play	_____	.
I	like	to	play	_____	.

Level 1: Glue each word on top of the printed word.
Level 2: Glue each word below the printed word.

I   like   to   play _____ .

By: _____

Level 3: No model. Cut and glue the words in the correct order.

Theme 6: I Like to Play

By: _____

soccer　　　　basketball　　　　baseball

tennis　　　　tag　　　　marbles

jacks　　　　hopscotch　　　　four-square

Theme 7: Things I Like

High-Frequency Words: I, like, my

Directions:

1. Refer to the procedures described on pages 5 and 6. Be sure to print each high-frequency word on an **index card** and review the words with the children prior to creating the cut-up sentence book.

2. Copy the **cut-up sentences** *(page 38)* and distribute them to the children in their envelopes.

3. Select the Level 1, 2, or 3 **reproducible book page** *(pages 39 and 40)* for each child. Choose the page according to the ability level of each child. Copy and distribute them to the children.

4. Copy the **book cover pattern** below. Have each child color, cut out, and glue the pattern onto a piece of construction paper. After the inside pages are complete, the cover can be added to finish the book.

5. Copy and distribute the reproducible **picture cards** *(page 41)*. Let the children use the cards as a reference for spelling and for choosing words to add to their stories. Alternatively, have the children select their own words to complete their stories.

Specific Ideas for Theme 7:

♦ "Things I Like" is the perfect theme for creating a predictable chart. Write the phrase "I Like" at the top of a sheet of chart paper. Model the first sentence with an example such as "I like my students." Write the sentence on the chart and put your name next to it. Ask each child to give a similar patterned response. Write each response on the chart paper with the child's name in parentheses next to the sentence. Make sure to track each word as it is read.

Example:

> I like my <u>bike</u>. *(Tom)*
> I like my <u>doll</u>. *(Ashley)*
> I like my <u>mom</u>. *(Bruce)*

Skills Practiced:

♦ Maintaining one-to-one correspondence
♦ Locating known and unknown words

Book cover pattern

Sentences for cut-up sentence book. See directions on page 37.

Theme 7: Things I Like

I	like	my	_____	.
I	like	my	_____	.
I	like	my	_____	.
I	like	my	_____	.
I	like	my	_____	.
I	like	my	_____	.
I	like	my	_____	.
I	like	my	_____	.
I	like	my	_____	.

Level 1: Glue each word on top of the printed word.
Level 2: Glue each word below the printed word.

Theme 7: Things I Like

I   like   my   _____ .

By: _____

By: _____

dolls

bike

trucks

teddy bear

friend

friend

Theme 8: My Family

High-Frequency Words: I, love, my, she, he, is

Directions:

1. Refer to the procedures described on pages 5 and 6. Be sure to print each high-frequency word on an **index card** and review the words with the children prior to creating the cut-up sentence book.

2. Copy the **cut-up sentences** *(page 43)* and distribute them to the children in their envelopes.

3. Select the Level 1, 2, or 3 **reproducible book page** *(pages 44 and 45)* for each child. Choose the page according to the ability level of each child. Copy and distribute them to the children.

4. Copy the **book cover pattern** below. Have each child color, cut out, and glue the pattern onto a piece of construction paper. After the inside pages are complete, the cover can be added to finish the book.

5. Copy and distribute the reproducible **picture cards** *(page 46)*. Let the children use the cards as a reference for spelling and for choosing words to add to their stories. Alternatively, have the children select their own words to complete their stories.

Specific Ideas for Theme 8:

♦ This is a great theme for teaching the pronouns *he* and *she*. Make a list of female family names: mom, mother, mommy, grandma, grandmother, granny, sister, sis, niece, aunt, and auntie. Also make a list of male family names: Dad, father, daddy, grandpa, papa, grandfather, uncle, nephew, and brother.

♦ Talk about various personality traits of the people in a family. Use words such as kind, fun, funny, silly, loving, and serious. Write these words on chart paper for the children to use in their sentences.

♦ The picture cards on page 46 can be made into a pocket chart learning center. Write the sentence structure: "I love my ___." on sentence strips. The students can read the sentence and fill in the blank by using the picture cards.

Skills Practiced:

♦ Exhibiting a return sweep
♦ Identifying and/or using capital letters

Book cover pattern

Sentences for cut-up sentence book. See directions on page 42.

Theme 8: My Family

I | love | my | _____ | .

She | is | _____ | .

I | love | my | _____ | .

She | is | _____ | .

I | love | my | _____ | .

He | is | _____ | .

I | love | my | _____ | .

He | is | _____ | .

Level 1: Glue each word on top of the printed word.
Level 2: Glue each word below the printed word.

I	**love**	**my**	______	**.**

(He or She)	**is**	______	**.**

By: ________________________

By: _____

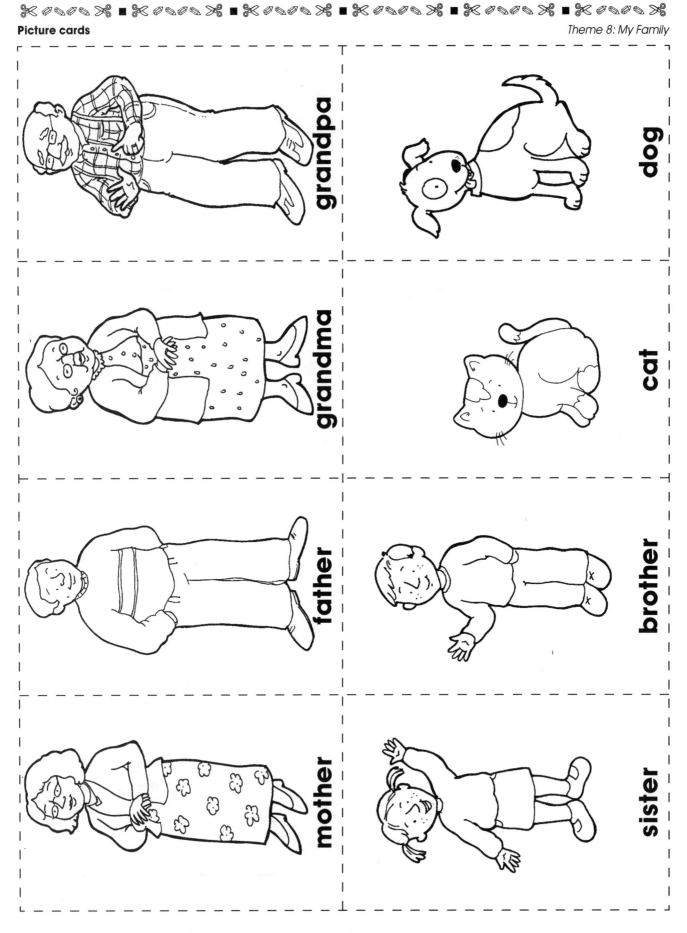

grandpa

dog

grandma

cat

father

brother

mother

sister

Theme 9: Environmental Print

High-Frequency Words: look, at, the

Directions:

1. Refer to the procedures described on pages 5 and 6. Be sure to print each high-frequency word on an **index card** and review the words with the children prior to creating the cut-up sentence book.

2. Copy the **cut-up sentences** *(page 48)* and distribute them to the children in their envelopes.

3. Select the Level 1, 2, or 3 **reproducible book page** *(pages 49 and 50)* for each child. Choose the page according to the ability level of each child. Copy and distribute them to the children.

4. Copy the **book cover pattern** below. Have each child color, cut out, and glue the pattern onto a piece of construction paper. After the inside pages are complete, the cover can be added to finish the book.

5. Copy and distribute the reproducible **picture cards** *(page 51)*. Let the children use the cards as a reference for spelling and for choosing words to add to their stories. Alternatively, have the children select their own words to complete their stories.

Specific Ideas for Theme 9:

◆ This is a wonderful theme to help boost the self-confidence of the children. Many kindergartners believe that they cannot read. This theme shows them that they already know how to read lots of words.

◆ Collect several different wrappers, labels, and food containers from familiar candies, toys, stores, and restaurants. When the children see the labels, they will be delighted that they are actually able to read (or recognize) so many words. Save the labels and place them in a learning center where the children can continue making sentences.

Skills Practiced:

◆ Identifying a word vs. a letter
◆ Knowing where to start and which way to go
◆ Recognizing that pictures help us read words

Book cover pattern

Sentences for cut-up sentence book. See directions on page 47.

Theme 9: Environmental Print

Look	at	the	_____	.
Look	at	the	_____	.
Look	at	the	_____	.
Look	at	the	_____	.
Look	at	the	_____	.
Look	at	the	_____	.
Look	at	the	_____	.
Look	at	the	_____	.
Look	at	the	_____	.

Level 1: Glue each word on top of the printed word.
Level 2: Glue each word below the printed word.

Theme 9: Environmental Print

Look   at   the   _____ .

By: _____

Level 3: No model. Cut and glue the words in the correct order.

Theme 9: Environmental Print

By: _____

newspaper

candy bar

cereal

book

Theme 10: Learning About Colors

High-Frequency Words: I, see, on, the

Directions:

1. Refer to the procedures described on pages 5 and 6. Be sure to print each high-frequency word on an **index card** and review the words with the children prior to creating the cut-up sentence book.

2. Copy the **cut-up sentences** *(page 53)* and distribute them to the children in their envelopes.

3. Select the Level 1, 2, or 3 **reproducible book page** *(pages 54 and 55)* for each child. Choose the page according to the ability level of each child. Copy and distribute them to the children.

4. Copy the **book cover pattern** below. Have each child color, cut out, and glue the pattern onto a piece of construction paper. After the inside pages are complete, the cover can be added to finish the book.

5. Copy and distribute the reproducible **picture cards** *(page 56)*. Let the children use the cards as a reference for spelling and for choosing words to add to their stories. Alternatively, have the children select their own words to complete their stories.

Specific Ideas for Theme 10:

◆ The theme "Learning About Colors" can be used for two different ability levels. First, use it at the beginning of the year. Block out the words "on the" and the second line on pages 54 and 55 so the children can only read "I see _____." Then have the children add a color word.

◆ Later in the year, when the children are more experienced with the concept of a return sweep, you can use the reproducible pages as they appear in this book.

◆ Creating the cut-up sentence book "Learning About Colors" is not only effective at the beginning of the year when the children are first learning to read color words, but this theme can also be revisited during a thematic unit on spring, rainbows, or St. Patrick's Day.

Skills Practiced:

◆ Recognizing that pictures can help us read words
◆ Maintaining one-to-one correspondence

Book cover pattern

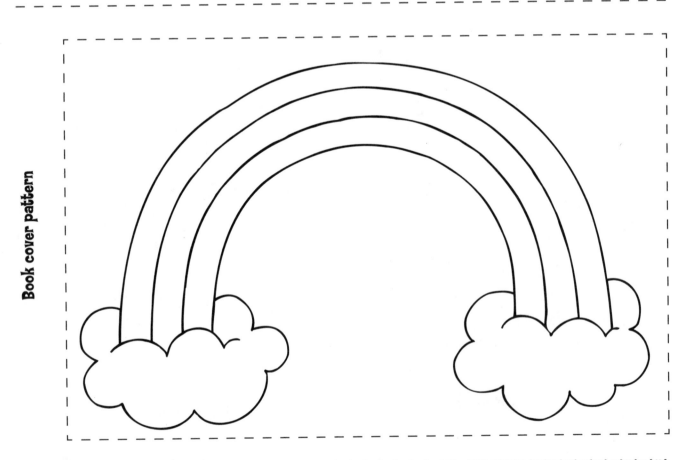

Sentences for cut-up sentence book. See directions on page 52.

Theme 10: Learning About Colors

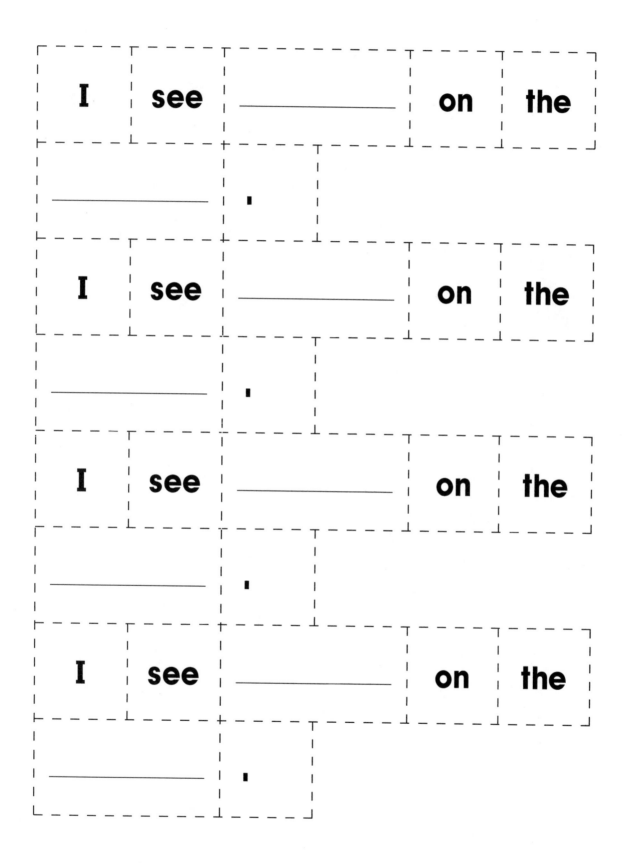

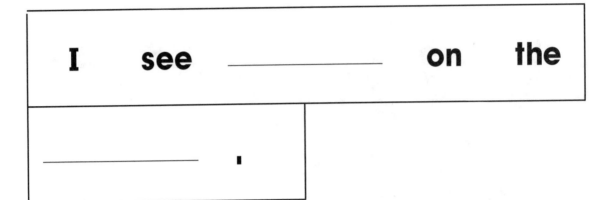

By: _____

Level 3: No model. Cut and glue the words in the correct order.

Theme 10: Learning About Colors

By: _____

red

blue

yellow

orange

green

purple

brown

black

white

Theme 11: Learning About Shapes

High-Frequency Words: this, is, a, an

Directions:

1. Refer to the procedures described on pages 5 and 6. Be sure to print each high-frequency word on an **index card** and review the words with the children prior to creating the cut-up sentence book.

2. Copy the **cut-up sentences** *(page 58)* and distribute them to the children in their envelopes.

3. Select the Level 1, 2, or 3 **reproducible book page** *(pages 59 and 60)* for each child. Choose the page according to the ability level of each child. Copy and distribute them to the children.

4. Copy the **book cover pattern** below. Have each child color, cut out, and glue the pattern onto a piece of construction paper. After the inside pages are complete, the cover can be added to finish the book.

5. Copy and distribute the reproducible **picture cards** *(page 61)*. Let the children use the cards as a reference for spelling and for choosing words to add to their stories. Alternatively, have the children select their own words to complete their stories.

Specific Ideas for Theme 11:

◆ Learning about shapes is generally part of math curriculum. Creating a cut-up sentence book about shapes helps children begin to understand that reading and writing are used in all areas of life, including math.

◆ Play the game, *I Spy*. The teacher says "I spy a (name of a shape)," and the children brainstorm all the things that they see in their classroom that are that shape.

◆ Divide a bulletin board into eight sections. Designate a shape to each section. Have the children draw or find pictures in magazines of shapes. Let the children tape them in the correct section of the bulletin board.

Skills Practiced:

◆ Maintaining one-to-one correspondence
◆ Looking for letter chunks: "is, this"

Book cover pattern

Sentences for cut-up sentence book. See directions on page 57.

Theme 11: Learning About Shapes

This	is	a	_____	▪
This	is	a	_____	▪
This	is	a	_____	▪
This	is	a	_____	▪
This	is	a	_____	▪
This	is	a	_____	▪
This	is	a	_____	▪
This	is	an	_____	▪
This	is	an	_____	▪

Level 1: Glue each word on top of the printed word.

Theme 11: Learning About Shapes

Level 2: Glue each word below the printed word.

This   is   a   _____ .

By: _____

Level 3: No model. Cut and glue the words in the correct order.

Theme 11: Learning About Shapes

By: _____

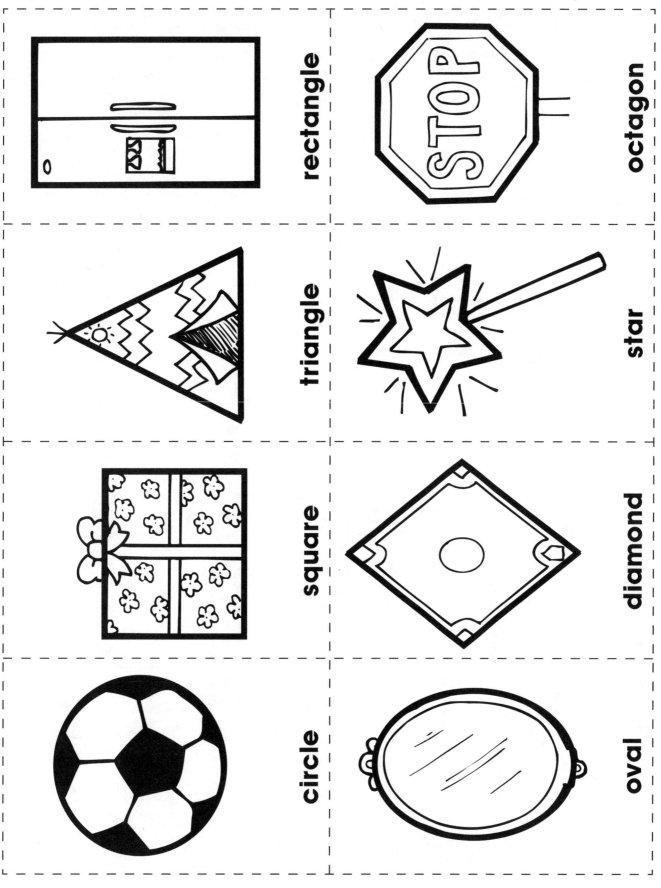

rectangle

octagon

triangle

star

square

diamond

circle

oval

Theme 12: What Is in My Lunch Box?

High-Frequency Words: what, is, in, my, a

Directions:

1. Refer to the procedures described on pages 5 and 6. Be sure to print each high-frequency word on an **index card** and review the words with the children prior to creating the cut-up sentence book.

2. Copy the **cut-up sentences** *(page 63)* and distribute them to the children in their envelopes.

3. Select the Level 1, 2, or 3 **reproducible book page** *(pages 64 and 65)* for each child. Choose the page according to the ability level of each child. Copy and distribute them to the children.

4. Copy the **book cover pattern** below. Have each child color, cut out, and glue the pattern onto a piece of construction paper. After the inside pages are complete, the cover can be added to finish the book.

5. Copy and distribute the reproducible **picture cards** *(page 66)*. Let the children use the cards as a reference for spelling and for choosing words to add to their stories. Alternatively, have the children select their own words to complete their stories.

Specific Ideas for Theme 12:

- This is an excellent theme for creating "flap" books. First, have each child sequence the cut-up sentence and glue it down. Then, instead of writing a food word on the blank, ask the children to draw a picture below the sentence of a food that they would like to have in their lunch box. Finally, tape a piece of paper over the picture so that it can be lifted up. The children will love reading the sentence and lifting the flap to discover what is in the lunch box.

- Many kindergartners have not had the experience of bringing a lunch to school. To make this reading experience more meaningful, ask the children to pretend that they are going on an imaginary trip. Ask the children what foods they would pack in their lunch boxes for this trip.

Skills Practiced:

- Exhibiting a return sweep
- Using different forms of punctuation (? and .)
- Looking for letter chunks: "wh" in what
- Knowing that questions require an answer

Book cover pattern

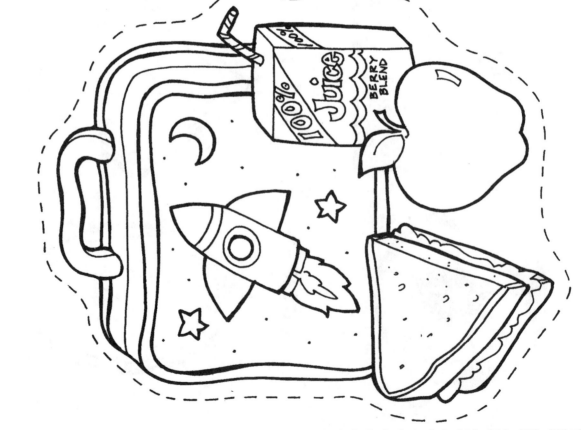

Sentences for cut-up sentence book. See directions on page 62.

Theme 12: What Is in My Lunch Box?

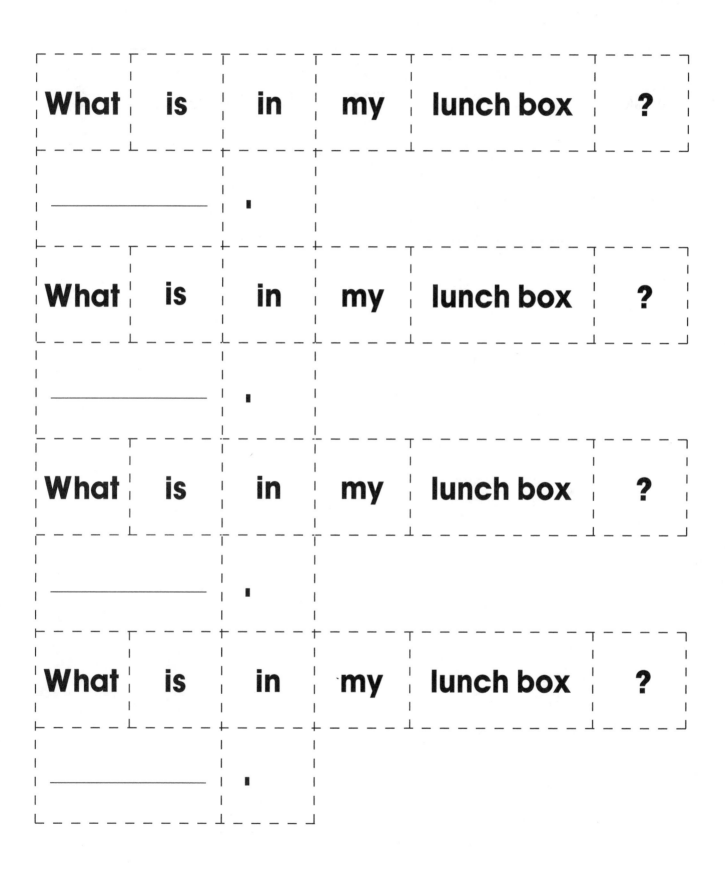

| What | is | in | my | lunch box | ? |

| ——————— | . |

| What | is | in | my | lunch box | ? |

| ——————— | . |

| What | is | in | my | lunch box | ? |

| ——————— | . |

| What | is | in | my | lunch box | ? |

| ——————— | . |

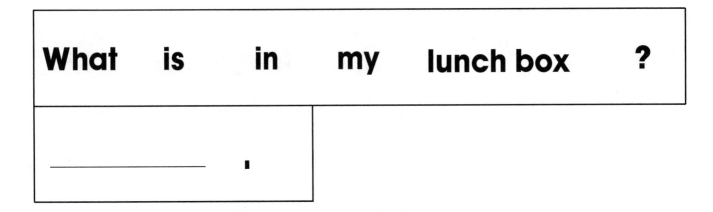
What   is   in   my   lunch box   ?

_____ .

By: _____

Level 3: No model. Cut and glue the words in the correct order.

Theme 12: What Is in My Lunch Box?

By: _____

Apple

Sandwich

Milk

Carrots

Pretzels

Yogurt

Theme 13: What Is in My Backpack?

High-Frequency Words: a, can, go, in, my

Directions:

1. Refer to the procedures described on pages 5 and 6. Be sure to print each high-frequency word on an **index card** and review the words with the children prior to creating the cut-up sentence book.

2. Copy the **cut-up sentences** *(page 68)* and distribute them to the children in their envelopes.

3. Select the Level 1, 2, or 3 **reproducible book page** *(pages 69 and 70)* for each child. Choose the page according to the ability level of each child. Copy and distribute them to the children.

4. Copy the **book cover pattern** below. Have each child color, cut out, and glue the pattern onto a piece of construction paper. After the inside pages are complete, the cover can be added to finish the book.

5. Copy and distribute the reproducible **picture cards** *(page 71)*. Let the children use the cards as a reference for spelling and for choosing words to add to their stories. Alternatively, have the children select their own words to complete their stories.

Specific Ideas for Theme 13:

◆ To create an interesting writing learning center, place a real backpack in the center along with pencils and paper. Ask the children to create lists of things they think should be in a backpack.

◆ Another fun idea is to copy the picture of the backpack below. Have each child color and cut out the pattern, spread glue along three sides of the backpack, and glue it onto another sheet of paper. The top edge of the backpack should be free of glue. Have the children draw, color, and cut out pictures of things that they would like to put in their backpacks. They can actually slide the pictures of these items into the tops of the backpacks. This interactive activity helps the children identify the words with the actual items.

Skills Practiced:

◆ Reading multi-syllabic words
◆ Re-reading to self-monitor
◆ Maintaining one-to-one correspondence

Book cover pattern

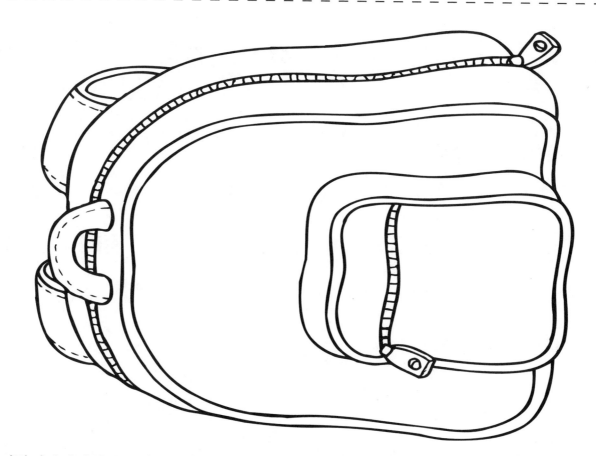

Sentences for cut-up sentence book. See directions on page 67.

Theme 13: What Is in My Backpack?

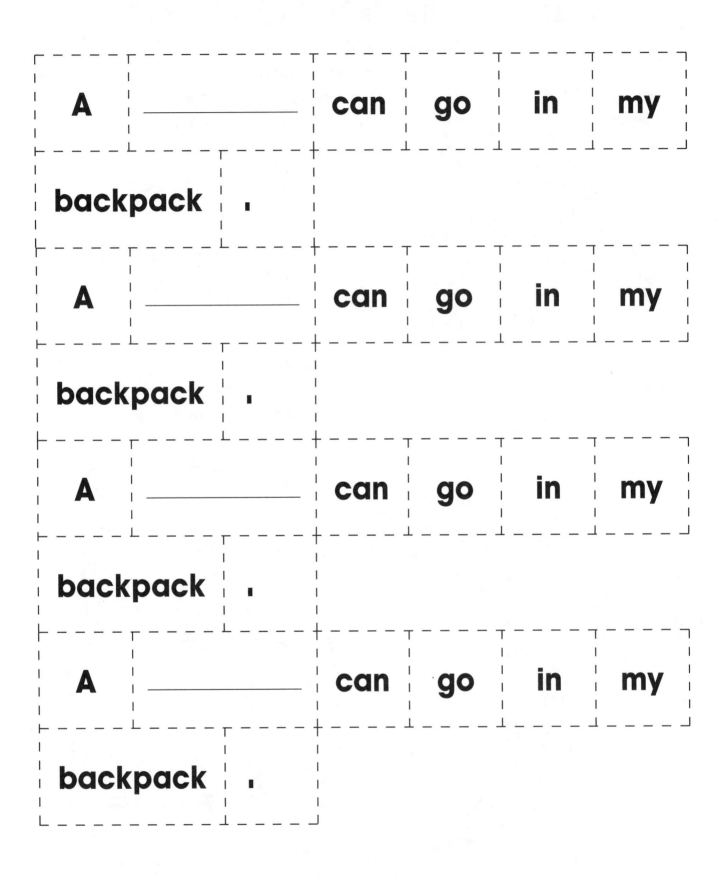

A _____ can go in my

backpack .

A _____ can go in my

backpack .

A _____ can go in my

backpack .

A _____ can go in my

backpack .

Level 1: Glue each word on top of the printed word.
Level 2: Glue each word below the printed word.

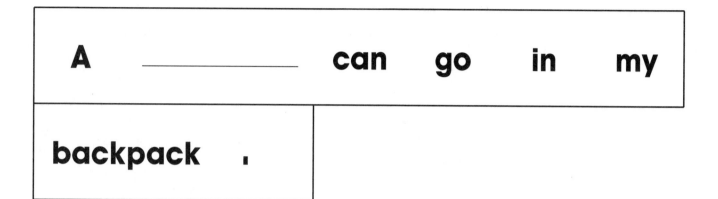

By: _____

Level 3: No model. Cut and glue the words in the correct order.

Theme 13: What Is in My Backpack?

By: _____

pencil

hat

scissor

book

pen

ball

Creating Cut-Up Sentence Books

Theme 14: Look at the Teddy Bears!

High-Frequency Words: here, is, a

Directions:

1. Refer to the procedures described on pages 5 and 6. Be sure to print each high-frequency word on an **index card** and review the words with the children prior to creating the cut-up sentence book.

2. Copy the **cut-up sentences** *(page 73)* and distribute them to the children in their envelopes.

3. Select the Level 1, 2, or 3 **reproducible book page** *(pages 74 and 75)* for each child. Choose the page according to the ability level of each child. Copy and distribute them to the children.

4. Copy the **book cover pattern** below. Have each child color, cut out, and glue the pattern onto a piece of construction paper. After the inside pages are complete, the cover can be added to finish the book.

5. Copy and distribute the reproducible **picture cards** *(page 76)*. Let the children use the cards as a reference for spelling and for choosing words to add to their stories. Alternatively, have the children select their own words to complete their stories.

Specific Ideas for Theme 14:

♦ Ask each child to bring in a teddy bear. Be sure to bring in several bears of your own, just in case some of the children do not have teddy bears. Ask each child to describe his or her bear. Is it big? Little? New? Soft? Fuzzy? What color is the bear?

♦ As a class, brainstorm a list of words that could be used to describe teddy bears. Write this list on chart paper and let the children use it as a reference when they work on their sentences.

♦ Math activities can be incorporated into this cut-up sentence theme book. The children can measure their bears and make comparisons of size, shape, and texture.

Skills Practiced:

♦ Reading multi-syllabic words
♦ Exhibiting a return sweep
♦ Re-reading to self-monitor

Book cover pattern

Sentences for cut-up sentence book. See directions on page 72.

Theme 14: Look at the Teddy Bears!

Here is a _____

teddy bear .

Here is a _____

teddy bear .

Here is a _____

teddy bear .

Here is a _____

teddy bear .

73

Here   **is**   **a**   _____

teddy bear .

By: _____

Level 3: No model. Cut and glue the words in the correct order.

Theme 14: Look at the Teddy Bears!

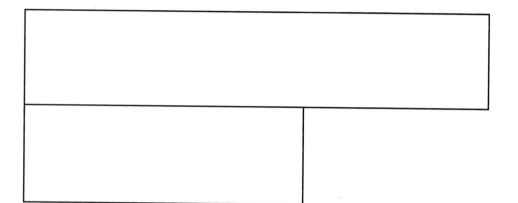

By: _____

big

little

soft

black

funny

furry

Theme 15: Farm Animals

High-Frequency Words: are, on, the, they, say

Directions:

1. Refer to the procedures described on pages 5 and 6. Be sure to print each high-frequency word on an **index card** and review the words with the children prior to creating the cut-up sentence book.

2. Copy the **cut-up sentences** *(page 78)* and distribute them to the children in their envelopes.

3. Select the Level 1, 2, or 3 **reproducible book page** *(pages 79 and 80)* for each child. Choose the page according to the ability level of each child. Copy and distribute them to the children.

4. Copy the **book cover pattern** below. Have each child color, cut out, and glue the pattern onto a piece of construction paper. After the inside pages are complete, the cover can be added to finish the book.

5. Copy and distribute the reproducible **picture cards** *(page 81)*. Let the children use the cards as a reference for spelling and for choosing words to add to their stories. Alternatively, have the children select their own words to complete their stories.

Specific Ideas for Theme 15:

♦ The farm animals cut-up sentence book can be used for two different ability levels. If return sweeps are still difficult, use only the first sentence: "_____ are on the farm." The children will only have to add the name of an animal. As the children become more proficient with return sweeps, you can add the second sentence: "_____ are on the farm. They say _____."

♦ Create a farm scene bulletin board. Use a store-bought bulletin board set or have the children make a farm mural. Place an index card next to each animal with the animal's name written on it. Draw a speech bubble for each animal and write the sound it makes. Review the animal names and sounds before starting the cut-up sentence books.

Skills Practiced:

♦ Using different forms of punctuation (" ")
♦ Identifying letter chunks: th (they, the), ck (ducks, quack)

Book cover pattern

Sentences for cut-up sentence book. See directions on page 77.

Theme 15: Farm Animals

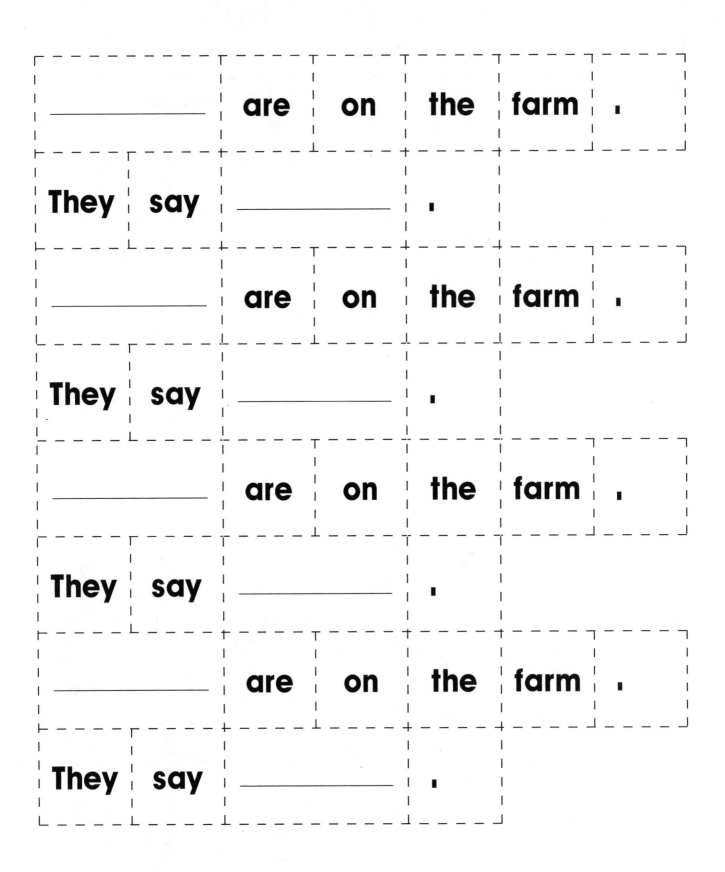

_____ | are | on | the | farm | .

They | say | _____ | .

_____ | are | on | the | farm | .

They | say | _____ | .

_____ | are | on | the | farm | .

They | say | _____ | .

_____ | are | on | the | farm | .

They | say | _____ | .

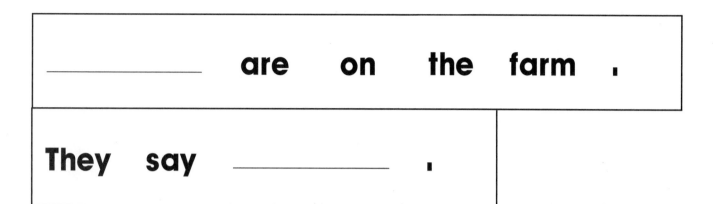

By: _____

Level 3: No model. Cut and glue the words in the correct order.

Theme 15: Farm Animals

By: _____

cows

cats

ducks

pigs

sheep

chickens

"moo"

"meow"

"quack"

"oink"

"baa"

"cluck"

Theme 16: Fun at the Zoo

High-Frequency Words: I, like, the, she, he, said

Directions:

1. Refer to the procedures described on pages 5 and 6. Be sure to print each high-frequency word on an **index card** and review the words with the children prior to creating the cut-up sentence book.

2. Copy the **cut-up sentences** *(page 83)* and distribute them to the children in their envelopes.

3. Select the Level 1, 2, or 3 **reproducible book page** *(pages 84 and 85)* for each child. Choose the page according to the ability level of each child. Copy and distribute them to the children.

4. Copy the **book cover pattern** below. Have each child color, cut out, and glue the pattern onto a piece of construction paper. After the inside pages are complete, the cover can be added to finish the book.

5. Copy and distribute the reproducible **picture cards** *(page 86)*. Let the children use the cards as a reference for spelling and for choosing words to add to their stories. Alternatively, have the children select their own words to complete their stories.

Specific Ideas for Theme 16:

◆ This theme can be used to make delightful "flap" books. Draw the outline of a cage and give each child a copy. Have the children glue the left edge of the cage onto a sheet of paper, leaving the right side free. The children can glue pictures of various animals under their cages. When they lift the flaps, they will be able to see the animals that they chose for their sentences.

◆ This "flap" book also makes a wonderful classroom big book. Each child, or pair of children, can make a large page (12" x 18") for the big book. Children will love reading this book all year long.

◆ Label a classroom zoo bulletin board with the names of the animals for the children to use as an independent resource.

Skills Practiced:

◆ Using different forms of punctuation
◆ Locating known words
◆ Maintaining one-to-one correspondence

Book cover pattern

Sentences for cut-up sentence book. See directions on page 82.

Theme 16: Fun at the Zoo

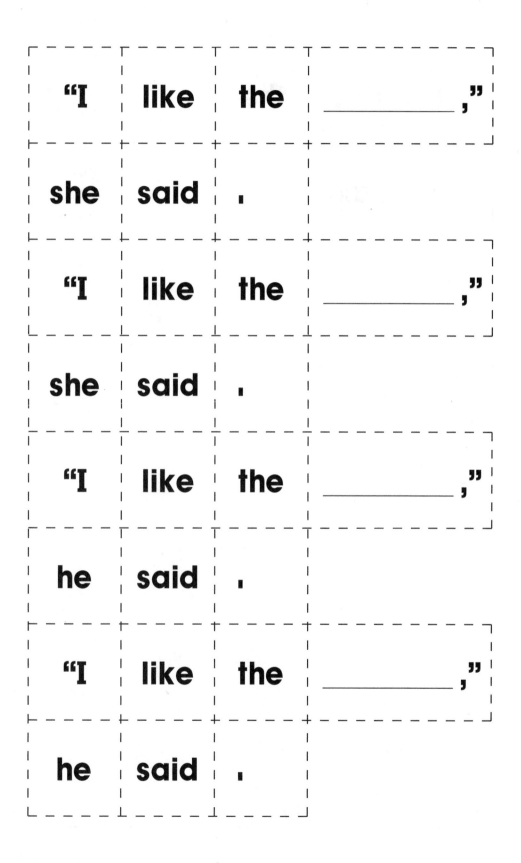

"I | like | the | _____ ,"

she | said | .

"I | like | the | _____ ,"

she | said | .

"I | like | the | _____ ,"

he | said | .

"I | like | the | _____ ,"

he | said | .

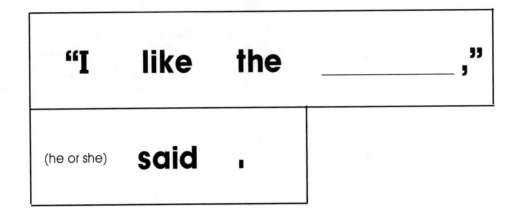

"I   like   the   _____,"

(he or she)   **said** .

By: _____

Level 3: No model. Cut and glue the words in the correct order.

Theme 16: Fun at the Zoo

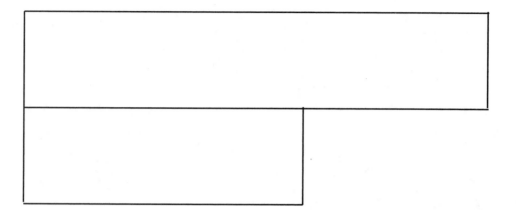

By: _____

lions

tigers

zebras

monkeys

elephants

seals

Theme 17: Look at the Bugs!
High-Frequency Words: I, see, a, it, is, on, the

Directions:

1. Refer to the procedures described on pages 5 and 6. Be sure to print each high-frequency word on an **index card** and review the words with the children prior to creating the cut-up sentence book.

2. Copy the **cut-up sentences** *(page 88)* and distribute them to the children in their envelopes. .

3. Select the Level 1, 2, or 3 **reproducible book page** *(pages 89 and 90)* for each child. Choose the page according to the ability level of each child. Copy and distribute them to the children.

4. Copy the **book cover pattern** below. Have each child color, cut out, and glue the pattern onto a piece of construction paper. After the inside pages are complete, the cover can be added to finish the book.

5. Copy and distribute the reproducible **picture cards** *(page 91)*. Let the children use the cards as a reference for spelling and for choosing words to add to their stories. Alternatively, have the children select their own words to complete their stories.

Specific Ideas for Theme 17:

◆ To add some excitement to this thematic reading and writing unit, go on a bug hunt and capture some real bugs to write about. Orally model the sentences as you talk about and look for real bugs. For example:

I see a <u>butterfly</u>. It is on the <u>flower</u>.
I see a <u>fly</u>. It is on the <u>dirt</u>.
I see a <u>ladybug</u>. It is on the <u>grass</u>.

◆ If you do capture any bugs, be sure to keep them in a container with plenty of fresh air, water, and grass. Only keep the bugs long enough to observe them and talk about them. Then set them free.

Skills Practiced:

◆ Identifying and/or using capital letters
◆ Reading multi-syllabic words (ladybug, beetle)
◆ Identifying small words within larger words ("cat" in caterpillar and "bee" in beetle)

Book cover pattern

Sentences for cut-up sentence book. See directions on page 87.

Theme 17: Look at the Bugs!

| I | see | a | _____ | . |

| It | is | on | the | _____ | . |

| I | see | a | _____ | . |

| It | is | on | the | _____ | . |

| I | see | a | _____ | . |

| It | is | on | the | _____ | . |

| I | see | a | _____ | . |

| It | is | on | the | _____ | . |

Level 1: Glue each word on top of the printed word.
Level 2: Glue each word below the printed word.

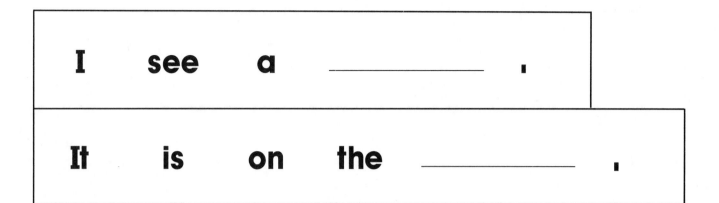

By: _____

Level 3: No model. Cut and glue the words in the correct order.

Theme 17: Look at the Bugs!

By: _____

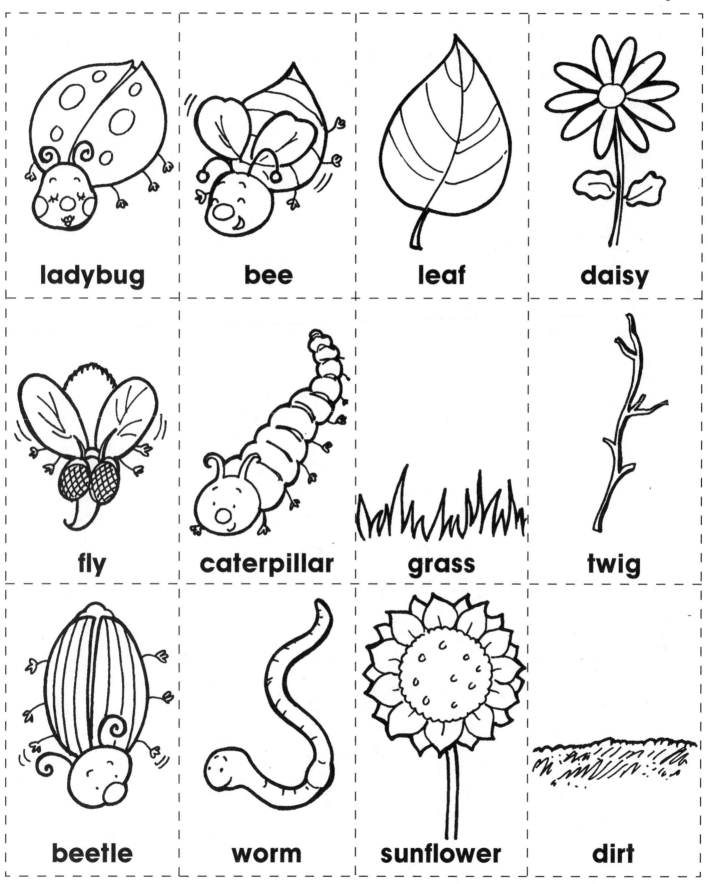

ladybug	**bee**	**leaf**	**daisy**
fly	**caterpillar**	**grass**	**twig**
beetle	**worm**	**sunflower**	**dirt**

Theme 18: Butterflies

High-Frequency Words: look, at, the, they, are, up, in

Directions:

1. Refer to the procedures described on pages 5 and 6. Be sure to print each high-frequency word on an **index card** and review the words with the children prior to creating the cut-up sentence book.

2. Copy the **cut-up sentences** *(page 93)* and distribute them to the children in their envelopes.

3. Select the Level 1, 2, or 3 **reproducible book page** *(pages 94 and 95)* for each child. Choose the page according to the ability level of each child. Copy and distribute them to the children.

4. Copy the **book cover pattern** below. Have each child color, cut out, and glue the pattern onto a piece of construction paper. After the inside pages are complete, the cover can be added to finish the book.

5. Copy and distribute the reproducible **picture cards** *(page 96)*. Let the children use the cards as a reference for spelling and for choosing words to add to their stories. Alternatively, have the children select their own words to complete their stories.

Specific Ideas for Theme 18:

◆ This theme is well-designed for introducing the concept of compound words. There are many compound words included in this theme: ladybug, butterfly, grasshopper, rainbow, and sunflower.

◆ Show the children how to fold a piece of paper in half and draw a "3" on the fold. Cut the paper along the outline of the "3" and open. The children will be able to actually see the symmetry of a butterfly. Add designs to the wings.

◆ Brainstorm with the children all the places that butterflies can be seen. Write the list on chart paper. After each idea, have a child come up and draw a picture of that place next to the word. The children may wish to use this list as an independent reference when they work on their cut-up sentences.

Skills Practiced:

◆ Identifying and/or using capital letters
◆ Reading multi-syllabic words

Book cover pattern

Sentences for cut-up sentence book. See directions on page 92.

Theme 18: Butterflies

Look	at	the	butterflies.	
They	are	up	in	the	_____ .
Look	at	the	butterflies.	
They	are	up	in	the	_____ .
Look	at	the	butterflies.	
They	are	up	in	the	_____ .
Look	at	the	butterflies.	
They	are	up	in	the	_____ .

Level 1: Glue each word on top of the printed word.
Level 2: Glue each word below the printed word.

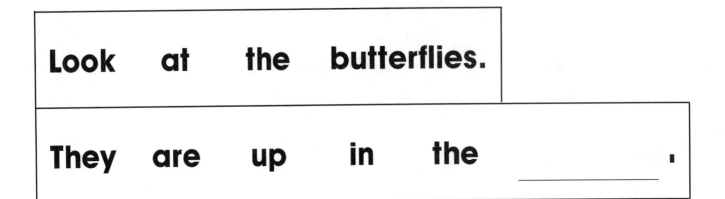

Look   at   the   butterflies.

They   are   up   in   the   _____ .

By: _____

Level 3: No model. Cut and glue the words in the correct order.

Theme 18: Butterflies

By: _____

tree

birdhouse

sky

flowers